THE 'ORIGINAL B[...]
OXFAM DIARY 2005

I thought: 'Bridget Jones' as soon as I heard the first extract – about the diet – from Ilene Powell's diary. We'd discovered it as part of a donation to our Cotham Hill shop in Bristol.

I loved the detail that Ilene gives about her life – the chaps, the dancing and the diets – and I knew lots of friends would too. I also thought the local newspaper might find the idea of a 'Bristol Bridget Jones' a good story.

Little did I think that 10 days later the story would be hot news across the world in newspapers and magazines as well as on national TV and the BBC World Service!

It's been a great end to the story to see the wonderful photos of the glamorous Ilene and to hear some of the colourful memories from an old friend, Nick Hastings. He confirmed that she was quite some lady, and would have been delighted with all the fuss, and that any money would be going to Oxfam!

I would like to thank Nick Hastings for his enthusiastic support.

Jen Brown,
Oxfam Bookshop Manager

The Real Ilene

We have just a tantalising three months' worth of entries in teenage Ilene Powell's diary. So what more do we know about her life?

Ilene was born on January 28, 1908, the youngest of six, one sister and four brothers, Lily, Frank, Arthur, Walter and Clarence.

She seems to have had a comfortable upbringing – enjoying a regular allowance from her father – a successful flour importer who seemed to enjoy indulging his daughter. She was a part-time dance teacher, an occasional fashion model and an amateur performer on the stage.

Despite the many eligible young men in her life, and a more regular boyfriend, Ilene spent quite a while as a singleton, marrying for the first and only time in 1940, at the age of 32. Unfortunately, it didn't last. Ilene and her husband, Jack Woodley divorced after the war, and he went to live in America, according to Nicholas Hastings, son of Ilene's best friend, who donated the diary to Oxfam.

After the divorce Ilene and her mother, Carole, ran a small 10-bedroom hotel in Clifton, Bristol called the White House. Being close to the BBC studios, it attracted a lot of theatre, film, and television people, including popular orchestra leader, Mantovani.

Nicholas Hastings remembers: 'She used to get up to a lot of things that I wouldn't want to go in to. I think she enjoyed her life very much – she was an absolute riot.'

When her mother died in the late 1960s, Ilene sold the hotel and bought a large house in Blackboy Hill, where she let rooms, later moving to Nailsea and then Clevedon, where she had a small flat.

Ilene died in hospital on May 17, 1985, aged 77. 'She was a feisty character and full of life right to the end,' recalls Nicholas Hastings.

Personal information

Name

Address

Postcode

Tel Fax

Mobile

Email

Doctor Tel

Blood group

Allergies

Dentist Tel

In emergency, contact

Name

Address

Tel

Important numbers

2004

JANUARY

M	T	W	T	F	S	S
			1	2	3	4
5	6	7	8	9	10	11
12	13	14	15	16	17	18
19	20	21	22	23	24	25
26	27	28	29	30	31	

FEBRUARY

M	T	W	T	F	S	S
						1
2	3	4	5	6	7	8
9	10	11	12	13	14	15
16	17	18	19	20	21	22
23	24	25	26	27	28	29

MARCH

M	T	W	T	F	S	S
1	2	3	4	5	6	7
8	9	10	11	12	13	14
15	16	17	18	19	20	21
22	23	24	25	26	27	28
29	30	31				

APRIL

M	T	W	T	F	S	S
			1	2	3	4
5	6	7	8	9	10	11
12	13	14	15	16	17	18
19	20	21	22	23	24	25
26	27	28	29	30		

MAY

M	T	W	T	F	S	S
					1	2
3	4	5	6	7	8	9
10	11	12	13	14	15	16
17	18	19	20	21	22	23
24	25	26	27	28	29	30
31						

JUNE

M	T	W	T	F	S	S
	1	2	3	4	5	6
7	8	9	10	11	12	13
14	15	16	17	18	19	20
21	22	23	24	25	26	27
28	29	30				

JULY

M	T	W	T	F	S	S
			1	2	3	4
5	6	7	8	9	10	11
12	13	14	15	16	17	18
19	20	21	22	23	24	25
26	27	28	29	30	31	

AUGUST

M	T	W	T	F	S	S
						1
2	3	4	5	6	7	8
9	10	11	12	13	14	15
16	17	18	19	20	21	22
23	24	25	26	27	28	29
30	31					

SEPTEMBER

M	T	W	T	F	S	S
		1	2	3	4	5
6	7	8	9	10	11	12
13	14	15	16	17	18	19
20	21	22	23	24	25	26
27	28	29	30			

OCTOBER

M	T	W	T	F	S	S
				1	2	3
4	5	6	7	8	9	10
11	12	13	14	15	16	17
18	19	20	21	22	23	24
25	26	27	28	29	30	31

NOVEMBER

M	T	W	T	F	S	S
1	2	3	4	5	6	7
8	9	10	11	12	13	14
15	16	17	18	19	20	21
22	23	24	25	26	27	28
29	30					

DECEMBER

M	T	W	T	F	S	S
		1	2	3	4	5
6	7	8	9	10	11	12
13	14	15	16	17	18	19
20	21	22	23	24	25	26
27	28	29	30	31		

2005

JANUARY

M	T	W	T	F	S	S
					1	2
3	4	5	6	7	8	9
10	11	12	13	14	15	16
17	18	19	20	21	22	23
24	25	26	27	28	29	30
31						

FEBRUARY

M	T	W	T	F	S	S
	1	2	3	4	5	6
7	8	9	10	11	12	13
14	15	16	17	18	19	20
21	22	23	24	25	26	27
28						

MARCH

M	T	W	T	F	S	S
	1	2	3	4	5	6
7	8	9	10	11	12	13
14	15	16	17	18	19	20
21	22	23	24	25	26	27
28	29	30	31			

APRIL

M	T	W	T	F	S	S
				1	2	3
4	5	6	7	8	9	10
11	12	13	14	15	16	17
18	19	20	21	22	23	24
25	26	27	28	29	30	

MAY

M	T	W	T	F	S	S
						1
2	3	4	5	6	7	8
9	10	11	12	13	14	15
16	17	18	19	20	21	22
23	24	25	26	27	28	29
30	31					

JUNE

M	T	W	T	F	S	S
		1	2	3	4	5
6	7	8	9	10	11	12
13	14	15	16	17	18	19
20	21	22	23	24	25	26
27	28	29	30			

JULY

M	T	W	T	F	S	S
				1	2	3
4	5	6	7	8	9	10
11	12	13	14	15	16	17
18	19	20	21	22	23	24
25	26	27	28	29	30	31

AUGUST

M	T	W	T	F	S	S
1	2	3	4	5	6	7
8	9	10	11	12	13	14
15	16	17	18	19	20	21
22	23	24	25	26	27	28
29	30	31				

SEPTEMBER

M	T	W	T	F	S	S
			1	2	3	4
5	6	7	8	9	10	11
12	13	14	15	16	17	18
19	20	21	22	23	24	25
26	27	28	29	30		

OCTOBER

M	T	W	T	F	S	S
					1	2
3	4	5	6	7	8	9
10	11	12	13	14	15	16
17	18	19	20	21	22	23
24	25	26	27	28	29	30
31						

NOVEMBER

M	T	W	T	F	S	S
	1	2	3	4	5	6
7	8	9	10	11	12	13
14	15	16	17	18	19	20
21	22	23	24	25	26	27
28	29	30				

DECEMBER

M	T	W	T	F	S	S
			1	2	3	4
5	6	7	8	9	10	11
12	13	14	15	16	17	18
19	20	21	22	23	24	25
26	27	28	29	30	31	

2006

JANUARY

M	T	W	T	F	S	S
						1
2	3	4	5	6	7	8
9	10	11	12	13	14	15
16	17	18	19	20	21	22
23	24	25	26	27	28	29
30	31					

FEBRUARY

M	T	W	T	F	S	S
		1	2	3	4	5
6	7	8	9	10	11	12
13	14	15	16	17	18	19
20	21	22	23	24	25	26
27	28					

MARCH

M	T	W	T	F	S	S
		1	2	3	4	5
6	7	8	9	10	11	12
13	14	15	16	17	18	19
20	21	22	23	24	25	26
27	28	29	30	31		

APRIL

M	T	W	T	F	S	S
					1	2
3	4	5	6	7	8	9
10	11	12	13	14	15	16
17	18	19	20	21	22	23
24	25	26	27	28	29	30

MAY

M	T	W	T	F	S	S
1	2	3	4	5	6	7
8	9	10	11	12	13	14
15	16	17	18	19	20	21
22	23	24	25	26	27	28
29	30	31				

JUNE

M	T	W	T	F	S	S
			1	2	3	4
5	6	7	8	9	10	11
12	13	14	15	16	17	18
19	20	21	22	23	24	25
26	27	28	29	30		

JULY

M	T	W	T	F	S	S
					1	2
3	4	5	6	7	8	9
10	11	12	13	14	15	16
17	18	19	20	21	22	23
24	25	26	27	28	29	30
31						

AUGUST

M	T	W	T	F	S	S
	1	2	3	4	5	6
7	8	9	10	11	12	13
14	15	16	17	18	19	20
21	22	23	24	25	26	27
28	29	30	31			

SEPTEMBER

M	T	W	T	F	S	S
				1	2	3
4	5	6	7	8	9	10
11	12	13	14	15	16	17
18	19	20	21	22	23	24
25	26	27	28	29	30	

OCTOBER

M	T	W	T	F	S	S
						1
2	3	4	5	6	7	8
9	10	11	12	13	14	15
16	17	18	19	20	21	22
23	24	25	26	27	28	29
30	31					

NOVEMBER

M	T	W	T	F	S	S
		1	2	3	4	5
6	7	8	9	10	11	12
13	14	15	16	17	18	19
20	21	22	23	24	25	26
27	28	29	30			

DECEMBER

M	T	W	T	F	S	S
				1	2	3
4	5	6	7	8	9	10
11	12	13	14	15	16	17
18	19	20	21	22	23	24
25	26	27	28	29	30	31

Easter Sunday 2006 – April 16

● new moon ○ full moon

27 Monday — Holiday: UK and Rep. of Ireland

28 Tuesday — Holiday: UK and Rep. of Ireland

29 Wednesday

30 Thursday

31 Friday

1 Saturday — New Year's Day

2 Sunday

3 Monday Bank Holiday: UK and Rep. of Ireland

4 Tuesday Holiday: Scotland

5 Wednesday

6 Thursday

7 Friday

8 Saturday

9 Sunday

10 Monday ●

11 Tuesday

12 Wednesday

13 Thursday

14 Friday

15 Saturday

16 Sunday

17 Monday

18 Tuesday

19 Wednesday

20 Thursday

21 Friday

22 Saturday

23 Sunday

Burns' Night

FOR LARGE,

24 Monday

25 Tuesday ○

26 Wednesday

27 Thursday — Holocaust Memorial Day

28 Friday

29 Saturday

30 Sunday

31 Monday

1 Tuesday

2 Wednesday

3 Thursday

4 Friday

5 Saturday

6 Sunday

7 Monday

8 Tuesday ●

Shrove Tuesday

9 Wednesday

Ash Wednesday

10 Thursday

11 Friday

12 Saturday

13 Sunday

14 Monday St. Valentine's Day

15 Tuesday

16 Wednesday

17 Thursday

18 Friday

19 Saturday

20 Sunday

21 Monday

22 Tuesday

23 Wednesday

24 Thursday ○

25 Friday

26 Saturday

27 Sunday

28 Monday

1 Tuesday — St David's Day

2 Wednesday

3 Thursday

4 Friday

5 Saturday

6 Sunday — Mothering Sunday

7 Monday

8 Tuesday International Women's Day

9 Wednesday

10 Thursday ●

11 Friday

12 Saturday

13 Sunday

14 Monday

15 Tuesday

16 Wednesday

17 Thursday

St Patrick's Day Holiday: Northern Ireland and Rep. of Ireland

18 Friday

19 Saturday

20 Sunday

HW 144

21 Monday

22 Tuesday

23 Wednesday

24 Thursday

25 Friday ○ Good Friday Holiday: UK except Northern Ireland

26 Saturday

27 Sunday British Summer Time begins Easter Sunday

28 Monday — Easter Monday Holiday: UK and Rep. of Ireland

29 Tuesday — Holiday: Northern Ireland

30 Wednesday

31 Thursday

1 Friday

2 Saturday

3 Sunday

4 Monday

5 Tuesday

6 Wednesday

7 Thursday

8 Friday ●

9 Saturday

10 Sunday

11 Monday

12 Tuesday

13 Wednesday

14 Thursday

15 Friday

16 Saturday

17 Sunday

Perso
Watch
Season
Telepho
Motor C
Motor D
Bank Pa
Holders
N.S.
Size in C
Size in
Size in C
Size in
Weight
Height
roughout
e times
cal data
for the
ation of
altered

1 Th—*Circumcision.* Stock Exchange closed
☽ First Quarter, 11.26 p.m.

Came home from London with Eddie Welsh by road after 5 weeks holiday in town, having stayed with Heatons, Gilders, & Snooks. Had lunch with the Levi's at Cricklewood, and tea at Reading. Met Mr Woodley in Reading café. Terrible gale across Salisbury Plain, stopped at Marlboro', home at 10 o'c. Eddie had supper here, & left at 11 o'c.

2 Fri This morning the boys (Bob, Bill and Mervyn) came up singing carols at side door soon after 11.30. Did not stop for lunch, coming up to tea tomorrow.

Molly's Birthday.

3 Sat The boys came up to tea today as usual (Bob, Bill, & Mervyn, also Claude.) Had a topping day. Bob's last day home. Bill & Bob went home early. Mervyn took me to White Ladies, and Claude brought Vera. Dennis took Uda. Mollie also was there, I gave her bottle of scent. We all thought the dance very good tonight.

4 Sun—2nd after Christmas

Clarie and I got up at 7 o'c this a.m. Walked to Temple Meads to see Bob & Bill off, and got there at 8 o'c. Bob off to Yorkshire for good, Bill to Glasgow for 3 weeks. Had a cab back. Hailing & raining. Car in dock so could not go out tonight.

5 Mon

I
did
her
day
Re

6 Tue

from
Wen
Eva,
Sutton,
to ls.
of N
who
to see
not be

18 Monday

19 Tuesday

20 Wednesday

21 Thursday

22 Friday

23 Saturday St George's Day

24 Sunday ○

25 Monday

26 Tuesday

27 Wednesday

28 Thursday

29 Friday

30 Saturday

1 Sunday

May **1** 2 3 4 5 6 **7** **8** 9 10 11 12 13 **14** **15** 16 17 18 19 20 **21** **22** 23 24 25 26 27 **28** **29** 30 31

2 Monday May Day Holiday: UK and Rep. of Ireland

3 Tuesday

4 Wednesday

5 Thursday

6 Friday

7 **Saturday**

8 **Sunday** ●

9 Monday

10 Tuesday

11 Wednesday

12 Thursday

13 Friday

14 Saturday

15 Sunday

5 Mon—Plough Monday. Dividends due

Intend going into town, but did not - rotten hellish cold in head.

Stayed indoors all day drawing ugly faces!

—

Read "the Harvester".

6 Tues—Epiphany Had a long letter from Bill today, written Sunday. Went in town with Mother, met Eva, had tea in Boots. Saw Frank Sutton in there & had a chat. Went to 1st house Colston Hall—"Hunchback of Notre Dame". We met two fellows who escorted us to Knowle cars. Promised to see one (George Baker) again but will not be doing so. Home before 9 o'c.

JANUARY, 1925.

7 Wed Clarrie heard from Bob.
I wrote to Bill today, long
letter.
Beautiful weather – like
Spring. Went for walk alone
in country.
Stayed at home this evening,
several people called,
turned in about 10 o'c.

8 Th Another day of
sunshine – beautiful weather,
Called to see Mrs Jackson this
afternoon about Dorothy's
lessons. Called into Nellie's and
stayed there all the afternoon
until 6.30 – Tried on all the
hats in the shop. Mum came
down to meet me.

Mai
9 Fri–
Hea
mon
Gave
lesson
'Shop
The d
up th
and
had a
until

10 Sa
Clarie
Vera
Jeanne
Prof: B
see M
Clarie,
Went to
Molli

16 Monday

17 Tuesday

18 Wednesday

19 Thursday

20 Friday

21 Saturday

22 Sunday

23 Monday ○

24 Tuesday

25 Wednesday — Africa Day

26 Thursday

27 Friday

28 Saturday

29 Sunday

Maison Jeanne

9 Fri—Christmas Fire Insurance ceases

Heard from Bill again this morning. Very long letter, 9 pages. Gave Dorothy Jackson dancing lesson this morning, 12-10's.

'Shopped' in Knowle this afternoon. The dancers from the old panto. came up this evening, also Dennis, Claude and Mervyn. I was rude to Claude, but had a good time. They did not leave until nearly 2.30 a.m.

10 Sat—If not already done, send in Accident Insurance Form. ○ Full Moon, 2.47 a.m.

Clarrie drove me to the centre to meet Vera this morning. We went to see Mde Jeanne, Park St. I had my hand read by Prof. Burgers. see P.D. Called into Bell's to see Mollie. Had coffee in oakroom with Clarrie, Mervyn, Dennis and Claude. Went to Corner House Thé Dansant with Mollie – very nice indeed.

11 Sun—*1st after Epiphany*

The boys drove us to White Ladies this afternoon – 1st rehearsal mannaquin parade, had some fun. Home at 6.30. Wrote to Bill.
Had a night in, doing odd jobs, but did not turn in until gone 10 o'c.

The boys took the 'Martels' to 'Ship'.

12 Mon—*Hilary Law Sittings begin*

Had a letter from Jack. (Reading)
Put off giving a lesson this morning. Had my hair waved. Went to White Ladies 12 o'c for rehearsal for mannaquin parade. Caught a worse cold and so could not be in it. George Baker 'phoned, wanted me to go out, but I didn't.
Vera 'phoned, but could not go out,
Went to bed early (10.30)

30 Monday — Spring Bank Holiday: UK

31 Tuesday

1 Wednesday

2 Thursday

3 Friday

4 Saturday

5 Sunday — World Environment Day

6 Monday ● Holiday: Rep. of Ireland

7 Tuesday

8 Wednesday

9 Thursday

10 Friday

11 Saturday

12 Sunday

13 Tues Morning 11 o'c.
Dancing Lesson, Dorothy Jackson.
– Ballroom. Took her home – felt ill. Called in to see Nell.
Bed very early tonight – still have a hellish cold "dans ma tête"
Bon soir.

---

14 Wed I now have lemon juice in hot water, mornings, with no sugar, instead of my first cup of tea, also apples before a very small breakfast of dry toast and weak tea – if this doesn't get my fat down I'll give up dieting!
Did not go out today.

JANUARY, 1925.

15 Th. Dorothy Jackson – a lesson @ 2.30 o.c.

Heard of Nora Hosegood's death – died last night.
Went in town shopping with Mother in morning – rotten weather.
Wrote to Bob in Yorkshire, and Walter Sanders (London)
Turned in 11.30.

16 Fri Town this morning – Pa said I could buy myself a pair of shoes, but did not spot a decent pair. Mrs Denman asked us to go to Hippo; but developed a cold, so went to see Colleen Moore in the "Perfect Flapper", also Edmund Lowe in "Honor among Men".
Met Mr George Baker this afternoon.

17 Sa
D
Met
Had
Clarie
awe
outsi
–promi
Bill hom
this e
Panto.

18 Su.
Ver
to te
let
calle
rheum
We
at 10.
J.G

13 Monday

14 Tuesday

15 Wednesday

16 Thursday
Father's Day World Refugee Day

17 Friday

18 Saturday

19 Sunday

20 Monday

21 Tuesday Longest Day

22 Wednesday ○

23 Thursday

24 Friday

25 Saturday

26 Sunday

27 Monday

28 Tuesday

29 Wednesday

30 Thursday

1 Friday

2 Saturday

3 Sunday

4 Monday

5 Tuesday

6 Wednesday ●

7 Thursday

8 Friday

9 Saturday

10 Sunday

Letter from Wallie (London)

17 Sat—☾ Last Quarter, 11.33 p.m.

D. J. a lesson at 10.oc.
Met Vera on centre at 11.15.
Had coffee in the Clare St cafe.
Clarie & Claude came in, also Mr Z
& wee wolfhound; we spoke to him
outside cafe. Met Jack Gough & —
-promised to go out tomorrow night.
Bill home this morning, came to see us
this evening - promised to take me to
Panto. dance at Spa Tuesday.

18 Sun—2nd after Epiphany

Vera, Mervyn & Bill came up
to tea. Jack Gough & Chapman
let us down. Will & Tony
called: Vera & I hid in front b. room
& heard the boys talking in bathroom.
Went out after them, Vera left
at 10.20. Clarie and the others saw
J.G with friends in Corner House.

JANUARY, 1925.

19 Mon D. J., a lesson at 12 o'c.
Bill phoned this a.m.
Shopped in town this afternoon with Mother, called upon Mrs Penman and Mrs Holland.

20 Tues Panto Cabaret Dance with Bill
Bill came up soon after 7 o'c; changed here; we left here at 9 p.m for Spa, had a taxi up. Enjoyed dance – over 400 people. Mum didn't come – Dad indisposed. Clarrie ran Bill & I home at 3.30 and we waited till 5 o'c for him, but he did not come. W.T.F.T.T.U.F.I.B's A.B.M. Kill it! Bill & I did not go to bed until gone 5. Clarrie came in at 6 o'c. heard 1st tramcar!!

21 We
Took
pus,
No. 6
Went
balls
3 gam
6 o'c.
6.30.
with
Bill we

22 Th
excep
and
Bill w
walke
with
Bill,
again
for
before

11 Monday Holiday: Northern Ireland

12 Tuesday

13 Wednesday

14 Thursday

15 Friday

16 Saturday

17 Sunday

18 Monday

19 Tuesday

20 Wednesday

21 Thursday ○

22 Friday

23 Saturday

24 Sunday

~~Today Mrs Elliot 'phoned.~~

JAN

o'c.

fternoon

ws

with
Bill

ne at
Enjoyed
didn't
n Bill &
o'c for
U.F.I.B's
to bed
'c. heard

21 Wed Got up before 12 o'c.
Took Bill in a cup of tea – at
which, a pillow fight ensued.
No breakfast – had lunch at 2 o'c.
Went along road to buy ping-pong
balls with Bill; came back & played
3 games (I won 1 only) Had tea at
6 o'c. Gave D.J. a dancing lesson at
6.30. After that, had a few dances
with Bill till Clarie came home.
Bill went at 8.30. & Clarie went to bed

22 Th No breakfast again today,
except for my usual lemon-water
and apple. Town this afternoon, met
Bill who waited while we shopped, and
walked from Wine St, to White Ladies
with us. Had tea in Picture House with
Bill, then left him to meet Mother
again at Mrs Hollands for fitting
for jumper suit-tunic. Home
before 9 o'c.

23 Fri Another late morning - in time for dinner stunt! Town this afternoon - home to give D.J. a lesson at 6.30. Conteau Elliot 'phoned, and came up this evening - home for a few hours only. Brought me a French silk scarf, bought in Havre; gave Mother a huge bottle of Eau de Cologne Ambrée. We went down to see him off - 11.50 train. Came back in ~~Mrs~~ Mrs Elliot's cab.

24 Sat — ● New Moon, 2.45 p.m. Letter from Ed. Daly

Went into town early this a.m. - had some shopping to do. Went to Mrs H's, came back, met Vera 11.30 on coathe, had coffee with Bill & Mervyn in oakroom café. Bill only was home to tea today - Clarie & Mervyn came home later, but went out again. Played T.T. and danced all the evening with Bill - quiet night - had a cold. Bill went at 11.

25 Su

Dinne
Go
went
Clarie,
Fairy,
out th
etc.
dresses
Bois:
miles.

26 Mo

25 Monday

26 Tuesday

27 Wednesday

28 Thursday

29 Friday

30 Saturday

31 Sunday

1 Monday Holiday: Scotland and Rep. of Ireland

2 Tuesday

3 Wednesday

4 Thursday

5 Friday ●

6 Saturday

7 Sunday

25 Sun—3rd after Epiphany.

Conversion of S. Paul

Jimmy Treen called.

Got up in time for dinner, but went back to bed afterwards. Clarie, Mervyn, & 2 Macs took Vera, Fairy, Uda & D.&P to ship. Mrs D. out there, also Ray, Lew, Jack Gough etc. Bill came up about 6 o'c, so I dressed. Went for a walk with him, to Bris: Westown, Red Lion etc - about 6 miles. Came home, played T.T. had supper, & Bill went at 10.30

26 Mon

27 Tues

28 Wed My 14th Birthday.

Had the usual greetings from everybody – on paper & otherwise. Bill 'phoned this a.m. Had slippers from Doris in Brum. I gave D.J a lesson at 6 o'c. Pen 'phoned; asked me to go to hear Peter Dawson & others at Police Concert tonight. Met Pen outside Colston Hall at 7.15. Spoke to Mr & Mrs Richards. V.G. Concert.

29 Th

Went
aftern
give a
Bill
night -
most of
in back
Clarie
cough

30 Fri

time fo
4.30,
Bill i
had tea
Left he
'The H
I saw

8 Monday

9 Tuesday

10 Wednesday

11 Thursday

12 Friday

13 Saturday

14 Sunday

15 Monday

16 Tuesday

17 Wednesday

18 Thursday

19 Friday ○

20 Saturday

21 Sunday

22 Monday

23 Tuesday

24 Wednesday

25 Thursday

26 Friday

27 Saturday

28 Sunday

29 Monday — Late Summer Holiday: UK except Scotland

30 Tuesday

31 Wednesday

1 Thursday

2 Friday

3 Saturday ●

4 Sunday

29 Th Did not get up this morning. Went into town with Mother this afternoon; came back in time to give a lesson at 6 o'c.

Bill brought his brother, Don, up to-night - expert T.T. player. We all played most of the evening. Had a few dances in back room before having supper. Clarie home tonight. The boys caught the last car home.

30 Fri Once again I get up in time for dinner. Went in town about 4.30, did a little shopping. Met Bill in Clare St. as arranged. We had tea in the Picture House with Mum. Left her & went up to White Ladies to see 'The Hunchback of Notre Dame'. I think I saw 'the world' in there tonight.

5 Monday

6 Tuesday

7 Wednesday

8 Thursday International Literacy Day

9 Friday

10 Saturday

11 Sunday

ot valid

p.m.

2 Mon—*Purification B.V.M. Candlemas.*

3 Tues 1st Pants Dance at Spa.
Clarie danced with Billie Goodwin
D.S.B with Terse, and
all evening with Denise St Ledger
to whom Clarie introduced him.
Good Dance. 11 till 3.30.
Bill came back here to
sleep. P.B.D!

12 Monday

13 Tuesday

14 Wednesday

15 Thursday

16 Friday

17 Saturday

18 Sunday ○

6 Fri

7 Sat Met Vera as usual, had coffee with the lads in the oakroom. Went to tea dance with Bill, Mollie Vera, Clarie & Mervyn. I danced with Jack Gough, Ken Hughes etc. Jack Woolley pinched car, and took me to White-Ladies. Danced with all the lads as usual, stopped Bill from going to the 'Old'. Had a good time, 6 people asked to take me home. There was a fight & Mrs Morgan fainted. Ticked off T.G. for making love to me on the roof garden. Home at 1.30 o'c

FEBRUARY, 1925.

8 Sun—*Septuagesima.* *Half Quarter Day.*
○ Full Moon, 9.49 p.m.

Got up soon after 11 o'c.
Mollie, Bill, Jack, and Mervyn came to tea. At 6.30 4 other boys called to take Mollie & I to 'Spiq's' 2 boys each! - Bryn. Hodges, Jack Gough, Charlie Chaplin & Rowles, Enjoyed ourselves, did 59 M.P.H. in Buick coming home. The boys came in and danced for an hr after 11 o'c, I beat Jack at table-tennis.
D.S.B.V.J.A.C.T.D.

9 Mon Jack Woodley called at 10 o'c this am to wish me goodbye before going back to Reading.

19 Monday

20 Tuesday

21 Wednesday International Day of Peace

22 Thursday

23 Friday

24 Saturday

25 Sunday

FEBRUARY, 1925.

12 Th Had my 1st dancing lesson since my visit to 'town' this a.m. and found that I was very stiff.
Bill phoned as usual, was yarning for half an hour.
Daley phoned to say he'd fetch me at 8.30 tomorrow in car.

13 Fri Yeomanry Ball with Daley

14 Sa
Met
usual
Bill h

15 Su

26 Monday

27 Tuesday

28 Wednesday

29 Thursday

30 Friday

1 Saturday

2 Sunday

3 Monday ●

4 Tuesday

5 Wednesday

6 Thursday

7 Friday

8 Saturday

9 Sunday

14 Sat—S. Valentine

Met Vera at 11.15 this a.m as usual. Had coffee in Oakroom, Bill looked in about 12 o'c.

15 Sun—Sexagesima

10 Monday

11 Tuesday

12 Wednesday

13 Thursday

14 Friday

15 Saturday

16 Sunday

17 Monday ○

18 Tuesday

19 Wednesday

20 Thursday

21 Friday

22 Saturday

23 Sunday

24 Monday — Holiday: Rep. of Ireland

25 Tuesday

26 Wednesday

27 Thursday

28 Friday

29 Saturday

30 Sunday — British Summer Time ends

18 Wed

19 Th Had my private lesson at 9.45 this morning. Town this afternoon, and dressmakers.
Bill took me to Competition dance at White Ladies, - quite good. Clarie & Heenagh brought Denise & Billie, They all came home here for another dance before finally clearing off.
Bill stayed the night here, we waited up alone for an hour. but no Clarrie so we went to bed.

31 Monday — Hallowe'en

1 Tuesday

2 Wednesday ●

3 Thursday

4 Friday

5 Saturday — Guy Fawkes' Night

6 Sunday

22 Sun—Quinquagesima

23 Mon—● New Moon, 2.12 a.m.

Got up at 11.30, Glorious day. Bill 'phoned. Did not go out anywhere today. Gave an hours lesson at 6 o'c.

FEB

FEBRUARY, 1925.

24 *Tues*—*Shrove Tuesday.* *S. Matthias*

25 *Wed*—*Ash Wednesday*

Went to Dancing at 9.30 - 12.o'c
- Students' Class.
Did not go out this
afternoon. Went to Triangle
with Bill this evening - had tea there.
Had letter and lost earrings from Terry
this morning.

26 Th

27 F

7 Monday

8 Tuesday

9 Wednesday

10 Thursday

11 Friday

12 Saturday

13 Sunday Remembrance Sunday

8 Sun—2nd in Lent

9 Mon Got up late today. Went out this afternoon, but not out of Knowle. Gave Dorothy a lesson at 6d. — till 1/4 to 4. Bill came up this evening. Played ping-pong in garage, I won two games & Bill the rest

10 Tue

11 We

9 —
Bi
him
to t
as
Sl
Had a
topping

14 Monday

15 Tuesday

16 Wednesday ○

17 Thursday

18 Friday

19 Saturday

20 Sunday

21 Monday

22 Tuesday

23 Wednesday

24 Thursday

25 Friday

26 Saturday

27 Sunday

10 Tues—○ Full Moon, 2.21 p.m.

11 Wed Dancing Lesson - Students, 9 - 12.45. Phew!
Bill phoned this afternoon. Met him in Oakroom, had tea, and went to the Triangle, - got in same bus as Teasse Patey. Saw the 'Sultan's Slave' - Claire Windsor - B. Lytell. Had another letter from Terry, also a topping little seed pearl choker necklace.

6 Fri

7 Sat

ut
out
lesson
ame
ping-
ive

28 Monday

29 Tuesday

30 Wednesday St Andrew's Day

1 Thursday ● World AIDS Day

2 Friday

3 Saturday

4 Sunday

MAR

14 Sat Met Vera as usual - stayed in saloon for an hour. Met Jack Gough & Ronks on centre. Went to W. Sydney tonight, had a lovely time. Danced with Bryn, Jack, Teddie Daley & others. Went to phone box down the road with B.H. while he 'phoned his mater. Four people would have brought me home, - came home in car with T.D. Our boys not at the dance, they went to Bassell races, then roamed around town. Bill played hockey at Corsham.

15 Sun—3rd in Lent.

Jack 'phoned to let me know that the boys could not come up - asked me to come out Wed. evening with Bryn. Mollie, Vera, & Bill came to tea. Had a lively time fighting the boys, dashing round the block of houses etc after blacking Bill's face with burnt corks. Bill drove Vera & Mollie home after giving them a scare at 11.45.

5 Monday

6 Tuesday

7 Wednesday

8 Thursday

9 Friday

10 Saturday Human Rights Day

11 Sunday

12 Monday

13 Tuesday

14 Wednesday

15 Thursday ○

16 Friday

17 Saturday

18 Sunday

MARCH, 1925.

16 Mon Bill 'phoned. – Wanted to put off Final Comp: dance at W. Ladies & go to W. Ward's dance at Grand. Coming up to see me tomorrow

17 Tues—S. Patrick. ☾ Last Quarter, 5.22 p.m.

Terry's Birthday.

19 Monday

20 Tuesday

21 Wednesday

22 Thursday
Shortest Day

23 Friday

24 Saturday

25 Sunday
Christmas Day

26 Monday

27 Tuesday

28 Wednesday

29 Thursday

30 Friday

31 Saturday

1 Sunday

2 Monday
Bank Holiday: UK and Rep. of Ireland

3 Tuesday
Holiday: Scotland

4 Wednesday

5 Thursday

6 Friday

7 Saturday

8 Sunday

2005 Year Planner

	Sa	Su	M	Tu	W	Th	F	Sa	Su	M	Tu	W	Th	F	Sa	Su	M	Tu
JAN	1	2	3	4	5	6	7	8	9	10	11	12	13	14	15	16	17	18
FEB				1	2	3	4	5	6	7	8	9	10	11	12	13	14	15
MAR				1	2	3	4	5	6	7	8	9	10	11	12	13	14	15
APR							1	2	3	4	5	6	7	8	9	10	11	12
MAY		1	2	3	4	5	6	7	8	9	10	11	12	13	14	15	16	17
JUN					1	2	3	4	5	6	7	8	9	10	11	12	13	14
JUL							1	2	3	4	5	6	7	8	9	10	11	12
AUG			1	2	3	4	5	6	7	8	9	10	11	12	13	14	15	16
SEP						1	2	3	4	5	6	7	8	9	10	11	12	13
OCT	1	2	3	4	5	6	7	8	9	10	11	12	13	14	15	16	17	18
NOV				1	2	3	4	5	6	7	8	9	10	11	12	13	14	15
DEC						1	2	3	4	5	6	7	8	9	10	11	12	13

2005 Year Planner

W	Th	F	Sa	Su	M	Tu	W	Th	F	Sa	Su	M	Tu	W	Th	F	Sa	Su
19	20	21	22	23	24	25	26	27	28	29	30	31						
16	17	18	19	20	21	22	23	24	25	26	27	28						
16	17	18	19	20	21	22	23	24	25	26	27	28	29	30	31			
13	14	15	16	17	18	19	20	21	22	23	24	25	26	27	28	29	30	
18	19	20	21	22	23	24	25	26	27	28	29	30	31					
15	16	17	18	19	20	21	22	23	24	25	26	27	28	29	30			
13	14	15	16	17	18	19	20	21	22	23	24	25	26	27	28	29	30	31
17	18	19	20	21	22	23	24	25	26	27	28	29	30	31				
14	15	16	17	18	19	20	21	22	23	24	25	26	27	28	29	30		
19	20	21	22	23	24	25	26	27	28	29	30	31						
16	17	18	19	20	21	22	23	24	25	26	27	28	29	30				
14	15	16	17	18	19	20	21	22	23	24	25	26	27	28	29	30	31	

Special dates

January

February

March

April

May

June

July

August

September

October

November

December

Addresses and phone numbers

Name

Address

Number

Name

Address

Number

Name

Address

Number

Name

Address

Number

Name

Address

Number

Name

Address

Number

Name

Address

Number

Name

Address

Number

Name

Address

Number

Name

Address

Number

Name

Address

Number

Name

Address

Number

Addresses and phone numbers

Name
Address

Number

Name
Address

Number

Name
Address

Number

Name
Address

Number

Name
Address

Number

Name
Address

Number

Name
Address

Number

Name
Address

Number

Name
Address

Number

Name
Address

Number

Name
Address

Number

Name
Address

Number

Addresses and phone numbers

Name
Address

Number

Name
Address

Number

Name
Address

Number

Name
Address

Number

Name
Address

Number

Name
Address

Number

Name
Address

Number

Name
Address

Number

Name
Address

Number

Name
Address

Number

Name
Address

Number

Name
Address

Number

International Dialling Codes

From the UK, dial 00 followed by the country code

Afghanistan	93
Albania	355
Andorra	376
Angola	244
Armenia	374
Australia	61
Austria	43
Azerbaijan	994
Bangladesh	880
Barbados	1246
Belgium	32
Belize	501
Bolivia	591
Bosnia and Hercegovina	387
Brazil	55
Burkina Faso	226
Burma (Myanmar)	95
Burundi	257
Cambodia	855
Canada	1
Chad	235
Chile	56
China	86
Colombia	57
Congo (Democratic Republic of)	243
Croatia	385
Denmark	45
Dominican Rebublic	1809
East Timor	670
Ecuador	593
Egypt	20
El Salvador	503
Eritrea	291
Ethiopia	251
Finland	358
France	33
Georgia	995
Germany	49
Ghana	233
Gibraltar	350
Greece	30
Grenada	1473
Guatemala	502
Guinea	224
Haiti	509
Honduras	504
Hong Kong	852
India	91
Indonesia	62
Iraq	964
Ireland	353
Israel	972
Italy	39
Japan	81
Kenya	254
Kosovo	381
Lebanon	961
Liberia	231
Luxembourg	352
Macedonia	389
Malawi	265
Mali	223
Mauritania	222
Mexico	52
Mozambique	258
Nepal	977
Netherlands	31
New Zealand	64
Nicaragua	505
Nigeria	234
Norway	47
Pakistan	92
Palestinian Territories	970
Peru	51
Philippines	63
Portugal	351
Russian Federation	7
Rwanda	250
St Lucia	1758
St Vincent	1784
Senegal	221
Serbia	381
Sierra Leone	232
Somaliland	252
South Africa	27
Spain	34
Sri Lanka	94
Sudan	249
Sweden	46
Switzerland	41
Tajikistan	992
Tanzania	255
Thailand	66
Uganda	256
United Kingdom	44
USA	1
Viet Nam	84
Yemen	967
Yugoslavia	381
Zambia	260
Zimbabwe	263

Notes

Notes

Notes

Notes

Notes

Notes